Und

Cialis

The Ultimate Guide to Deal with Erectile Dysfunction (ED), Premature Ejaculation, and Have a Long Lasting Sex

Nicholas Baker

Title | Understanding CIALIS
Author | Nicholas Baker
ISBN | 979-12-22763-35-4

Youcanprint
Via Marco Biagi 6, 73100 Lecce
www.youcanprint.it
info@youcanprint.it

Copyright © 2024 Nicholas Baker

All rights reserved. No part of this publication may be reproduced, distributed, or transmitted in any form of by any means, including photocopying, recording or other electronic or mechanical methods, without the prior written permission of the publisher, except in the case of brief quotations embodied in critical reviews and certain other noncommercial uses permitted by copyright law.

Legal Disclaimer

The information provided in this book, "Understanding Cialis, The Ultimate Guide to Deal with Erectile Dysfunction (ED), Premature Ejaculation, and Have a Long-Lasting Sex", is for general informational and educational purposes only. The author, Nicholas Baker, is not a licensed medical professional, and the content should not be considered a substitute for professional medical advice, diagnosis, or treatment.

Readers are encouraged to consult with their healthcare provider or a qualified medical professional before engaging in any treatment, especially if they have pre-existing health conditions or concerns.

Table of Contents

Chapter 1: Everything about Cialis 7
    What is Cialis? 7
    Properties of Cialis (Tadalafil) 10
    Is it safe to use? 11

Chapter 2: What is Cialis Used to Treat? 13
    Erectile Dysfunction 13
    Benign Prostatic Hyperplasia (BPH) 14
    Pulmonary Arterial Hypertension (PAH) 15

Chapter 3: Warnings and Precautions 17
    What to know before using Cialis 17
    Who can and cannot use Cialis 23
    Interactions 23

Chapter 4: Mechanism of Action 32
    How does Cialis Work? 32
        Duration 36
    Pharmacodynamics 36
    Pharmacokinetics 37

Chapter 5: Dosage and Side Effects 39
    The Right Dosage and Timing is Fundamental 39
        Dosage for Erectile Dysfunction 40
    Main Side Effects 43

Chapter 6: Frequently Asked Questions 52
Conclusion 56

Chapter 1: Everything about Cialis

What is Cialis?

Cialis is a medication that is only accessible with a medical recipe and goes by its brand name. According to the instructions provided by the FDA, it may be used to treat the following disorders in males:

- Erectile dysfunction, more often referred to as ED, is a condition in which a person is unable to develop or keep an erection. This may be a trouble for the pair.
- Signs of benign prostatic hyperplasia (BPH), a condition of the prostate that, if left untreated, may cause difficulties urinating and lead to other urinary problems.
- ED in addition to the other signs and symptoms of BPH.

Cialis is available in the form of a pill, which should be taken by mouth and consumed in its whole. You will need to take the medicine either just before participating in sexual activity or on a regular basis, depending on the severity of your condition and how often you engage in sexual activity. Cialis is designed to treat erectile dysfunction.

Tadalafil is the active pharmacological component of Cialis; this chemical is known as a phosphodiesterase 5 (PDE5) inhibitor. Cialis works by relaxing the blood vessels that go to the penis, which enables an increase in the quantity of blood that can flow into the penis. This results in an improved sexual experience. By relaxing the muscles in your bladder, Cialis may alleviate the symptoms of benign prostatic hyperplasia (BPH), making it simpler for you to urinate.

If a man's penis does not harden and expand when he gets sexually aroused or if he is unable to keep an erection going for more than a few minutes, we say that he has an erectile dysfunction. When a man is sexually stimulated, it is normal for his body to react by boosting the flow of blood to his penis in order to produce an erection. This is because the penis is the area of his body that responds to sexual stimulation. An increase in the amount of blood that flows to the penis is one of the effects that may be expected from taking tadalafil, which acts by blocking an enzyme. The patient is able to maintain an erection even after the penis has been stroked thanks to this treatment. It is not feasible for tadalafil to function to create an erection in the absence of direct physical stimulation to the penis, such as that which happens while sexual activity is taking place.

This treatment is reserved for men (BPH). BPH is caused by an enlarged prostate, which is the primary symptom. Most of the time, men who have BPH have trouble passing urine, have a decreased flow of urine, have hesitation at the beginning of the urination process, and have to get up in the middle of the night to urinate. Tadalafil will minimize the intensity of these symptoms, and it will also decrease the risk that prostate surgery will be necessary as a result of these symptoms.

Tadalafil is also used to treat the symptoms of pulmonary arterial hypertension, which may increase a person's capacity for physical activity and make it easier for them to exercise. Either females or males can use this method. The main artery, which is responsible for delivering blood from the ventricle on the right side of the heart to the lungs on the left side of the body, is impacted by this kind of hypertension. Tadalafil targets the PDE5 enzyme, which is located in the lungs, in order to relax the blood vessels that carry blood across the body. Because of this, the amount of blood that flows to the lungs will rise, and at the same time, the strain placed on the heart will decrease.

Properties of Cialis (Tadalafil)

Cialis is the trade name for tadalafil, a phosphodiesterase type 5 (PDE5) inhibitor primarily used to treat erectile dysfunction (ED), benign prostatic hyperplasia (BPH), and pulmonary arterial hypertension (PAH). Introduced by Eli Lilly and Company, it is considered a long-acting PDE5 inhibitor compared to its counterparts, such as sildenafil (Viagra) and vardenafil (Levitra).

Pharmacological Class

Cialis belongs to the class of drugs known as PDE5 inhibitors. These medications are designed to selectively inhibit the action of the enzyme phosphodiesterase type 5 (PDE5), which is highly concentrated in the corpus cavernosum of the penis, as well as in vascular smooth muscle cells of the lungs.

Mechanism of Action

The primary mode of action of Cialis involves enhancing the effect of nitric oxide (NO), a naturally occurring molecule involved in the regulation of vascular tone and blood flow. During sexual stimulation, nitric oxide is released in the corpus cavernosum of the penis, leading to the production of cyclic guanosine monophosphate (cGMP). cGMP mediates the relaxation of smooth muscle tissue and vasodilation (widening of blood vessels), which allows increased blood flow into the corpus cavernosum, ultimately resulting in an erection.

Tadalafil, by inhibiting PDE5, prevents the breakdown of cGMP. As a result, levels of cGMP remain elevated for longer, prolonging vasodilation and improving erectile function.

It's crucial to note that Cialis is not an aphrodisiac and requires sexual stimulation to be effective. The drug does not initiate an erection but facilitates the physiological process of erection by enhancing the body's natural response to sexual arousal.

Is it safe to use?

Cialis is often considered a drug that has a minimal risk of causing unwanted side effects. However, you should keep in mind the other medications that you take at the same time as this one, as well as the possible negative effects that might be brought on by the interaction of all of the medicines. The Food and Drug Administration (FDA) first granted permission for its use in ED in the year 2003, and then again, in the year 2009, it granted clearance for its use in PAH. In comparison to other PDE5 inhibitors such as sildenafil, tadalafil half-life is much longer, and it exhibits a higher level of selectivity for the enzyme PDE5. In addition, tadalafil has a higher affinity for the enzyme PDE5. As a direct result of this, tadalafil has developed into a more workable option for the treatment of PAH when it is administered once daily over a considerable amount of time.

Chapter 2: What is Cialis Used to Treat?

Erectile Dysfunction

Erectile dysfunction is defined by a multitude of symptoms, one of which is a man's inability to acquire or sustain an erection. Different aspects, including genetics and lifestyle, may cause this difficulty. When blood pours into a man's penis and pools there for an extended amount of time, this is regarded to be the beginning of an erection. This occurs as a result of the blood vessels and muscles in the penis relaxing and opening up, which permits an increase in the quantity of blood that flows into the region. In addition to this, this takes place as a consequence of an increase in the volume of blood that is carried out from the area. Your body creates a molecule that is known as cyclic guanosine monophosphate or GMP for short. One of its effects is to relax the muscles of the penis, which in turn promotes an increase in the amount of blood that flows to that part of the body.

Phosphodiesterase 5 (PDE5) inhibitors are a kind of therapy for erectile dysfunction, and Cialis is a member of the class of drugs that fall under this category. This is accomplished by the inhibition of PDE5, which is the primary factor in erectile dysfunction (ED). When PDE5 is inhibited, there is a subsequent increase in the amount of cyclic GMP that is produced by the body. You will find that the blood vessels and muscles of your penis become more relaxed whenever there is an increase for cyclic GMP in your system. Because of this, a greater flow of blood is permitted, which in the end leads there to be an erection.

Benign Prostatic Hyperplasia (BPH)

An enlargement of the prostate gland characterizes the disorder known as BPH, which does not contain malignant alterations, which is one of its symptoms. Urinary issues may be an indicator of benign prostatic hyperplasia (BPH), and the symptoms of this condition may include the need to pee often or the impulse to urinate more frequently during the night.

The Food and Medicine Administration has approved Cialis for use in the treatment of symptoms related with BPH; nevertheless, it is not fully known how the drug works to treat these symptoms and remove them. It is possible that Cialis works by relaxing the muscles in your bladder, which would make it easier for you to pee as a side effect of taking the prescription.

Pulmonary Arterial Hypertension (PAH)

Pulmonary arterial hypertension, often known as PAH and referred to in certain circles as simply PAH, is a potentially fatal ailment that is defined by an unusually high blood pressure in the pulmonary artery. This dangerous condition worsens with time. This artery is responsible for the flow of blood in both directions between the heart and the lungs since it connects the two organs and goes from one to the other. PAH is brought on by a constriction of the minute blood arteries in the lungs, which leads to a buildup of pressure and subsequently backflow of blood. Patients who have right-sided heart failure develop the condition as a result of their hearts' inability to keep up with the additional effort required to pump blood through the lungs over the course of their lifetimes. As a direct consequence of this, the right side of the heart loses its ability to perform its normal functions.

Primary or idiopathic PAH is the name given to this specific kind of PAH. It is also possible for PAH to develop as a secondary complication of other disorders, such as congenital heart disease, HIV, or illnesses of the connective tissue. PAH may cause a broad variety of symptoms, some of which include weariness, lightheadedness, trouble breathing, discomfort in the chest, and an erratic heartbeat. PAH can also cause a person's heartbeat to become irregular. If the patient's condition continues to deteriorate, the severity of their symptoms may eventually reach a point where they make it impossible for them to participate in any kind of physical activity.

Oral administration of the medication tadalafil, which has been given the go-ahead for usage in the treatment of PAH, is possible with tadalafil. Patients with PAH who took part in a clinical study that compared tadalafil to a placebo found that taking 40 milligrams of tadalafil per day improved the patients' functional abilities as well as their quality of life.

Chapter 3: Warnings and Precautions

What to know before using Cialis

When using this drug, there are a variety of different preventative measures that should be taken. Cialis therapy should not begin until you and your healthcare practitioner have had a discussion about your medical history.

Concerns relating to the patient's heart. It's possible that engaging in sexual activity will impact how effectively your heart functions. These problems might present in a number of different ways, such as a heart attack or an irregular cardiac rhythm, for example. Your primary care physician is in the greatest position to evaluate the state of your cardiovascular system and provide you with guidance on whether or not it is healthy enough to support sexual activity. You should immediately stop any sexual activity and seek an appointment with a medical practitioner as soon as you can if, while taking

Cialis, you have symptoms such as pain in the chest or an irregular heartbeat.

Pulmonary artery hypertension is also known as PAH. If you have pulmonary hypertension, which is a kind of high blood pressure that develops in the lungs, you should see your primary care physician before taking Cialis. This is because pulmonary hypertension may cause serious side effects. It is likely that the medication known as riociguat (Adempas) is what you are using to treat your pulmonary hypertension, but this is not usually the case. In addition, using this medication with Cialis may result in a reduction in your blood pressure that is at a level that might be life-threatening. Patients being treated for pulmonary hypertension with riociguat should not use Cialis since the two medications interact negatively.

Blood pressure concerns. There have been reports of Cialis users experiencing both high and low blood pressure while using the medication. Cialis has the potential to significantly exacerbate the symptoms of any of these conditions that you may already have. You should see your physician and discuss about your medical profile before beginning treatment with Cialis. During the course of your therapy, it is likely that they may give you the instruction to monitor your blood pressure more often to ensure that it does not reach levels that are either dangerously high or dangerously low.

Stroke. Taking Cialis may put you at an increased risk of having a stroke, particularly if you had a history of the disease in the past. Studies that were conducted after the FDA gave its approval for Cialis, indicated that some people who had a history of cardiac difficulties also experienced strokes.

Liver problems. This implies that the medicine may build in your system, which may enhance the risk that you may have undesirable consequences as a result of taking the prescription. It is conceivable that they will start you out on a low dose as a precautionary measure.

Problems with the kidneys. This might cause unwanted side effects. This suggests that there is a risk that the medication may collect in your body, which may result in some extremely significant negative side effects. Before commencing therapy with Cialis, you should discuss any kidney problems with your treating physician. It is conceivable that they may advise you to start taking the medication at a low dose as your first course of treatment.

A significant impairment to one's ability to see. Before commencing therapy with Cialis, you should first consult with your primary care physician about your previous experiences with vision loss. Vision issues, such as non-arteritic anterior ischemic optic neuropathy, are only one example of the kinds of conditions that might be contributing factors in this vision loss (NAION). If you already have vision issues, using Cialis may put you at an increased risk for developing further vision issues in the future. It is conceivable that your doctor may recommend a medication that is different from Cialis.

Retinitis pigmentosa. If you have retinitis pigmentosa, an inherited eye condition that may result in vision loss, you should not take Cialis since it might worsen your condition. Taking Cialis when you already have vision loss may raise the probability that you may have further visual side effects from the medication. It is conceivable that your doctor may recommend a medication that is different from Cialis.

Stomach ulcers. There is a good chance that using Cialis will increase the risk of bleeding that you already have. Before starting therapy with Cialis, you should see your primary care physician if you have a previous medical history that includes stomach ulcers. It is conceivable that they will recommend a different kind of therapeutic approach.

Issues affecting the flow of blood. Consult your physician before commencing therapy with Cialis if you have a previous medical history that includes problems with bleeding

Peyronie's illness or a penis deformity might be the root of the problem. If you have a history of Peyronie's disease, which is characterized by a bent penis, you should tell your healthcare practitioner. If you take the drug, there is a greater possibility that you may have an erection that lasts for a longer length of time than you would have otherwise. It is possible for blood to get entrapped in the penis, which may lead to an erection that lasts for more than four hours at a time. This disease is dangerous and has the ability to lead to long-term damage. It is possible that your doctor will urge you to take a low dose of Cialis or to make careful use of the prescription medication.

An investigation on the history of erections that persisted for more than 3 hours in the past. If you have a history of prolonged erections or priapism, there is a potential that using Cialis might boost your risk of developing these disorders while you are taking the prescription. This kind of erection is known as protracted. Priapism, on the other hand, is distinguished by an erection that is excruciatingly painful and that lasts for more than six hours. Both of these predicaments are considered to be emergencies and need quick care in order to lessen the severity of any possible long-term consequences. Consult your physician about your medical profile before beginning treatment with Cialis. It is possible that they will tell you to undertake careful monitoring of your condition after you have taken Cialis.

Problems with the blood cells. Ticklish cell anemia and other forms of blood cancer, such as multiple myeloma and leukemia, are only two examples of the several kinds of blood cell abnormalities that may develop. Before commencing therapy with Cialis, you should discuss any concerns you have about your blood cells with your treating physician. When you take the drug, there is a greater possibility that you may have an erection that lasts for a longer length of time than it would normally. Long-lasting erections that last longer than four hours provide a danger to one's health and have the potential to cause damage that cannot be undone. In the event that you are having issues with your blood cells, your physician can recommend that you take a low dose of Cialis.

Reactions brought on by allergic reactions. If you have ever had an adverse reaction to any of the components in Cialis, including Cialis itself, you should not take Cialis since it might make your condition worse.

Pregnancy. There has been neither an evaluation nor an authorization for the use of Cialis in female patients.

Breastfeeding. There has been neither an evaluation nor an authorization for the use of Cialis in female patients. There is no evidence about safety of this medication if taken while breastfeeding a child.

Who can and cannot use Cialis

Cialis should not be used by:

- Patients using nitrates.
- Individuals who have previously had an adverse response to Cialis or tadalafil.
- Individuals who use guanylate cyclase stimulators (riociguat.i.e.)

Interactions

Cialis has the potential to have a harmful interaction with a variety of other medications. Additionally, it may cause a reaction when used with some meals. One single interaction might potentially result in a great many different results. Some interactions, for instance, have the potential to reduce the efficacy of a medication, while others may have no impact. There is a possibility that other combinations will result in a higher number of adverse effects or a more severe manifestation of those effects. Cialis might potentially cause a negative interaction with the medications that are mentioned below. Cialis may have a potentially harmful interaction with a number of other drugs, some of which are not included on this list. Before commencing therapy with Cialis, you should first speak with both your primary care physician and your pharmacist. Give them a complete list of all the drugs you take, including those that you got with a prescription and those that you got without a prescription. Give them as much information as you can on the vitamins, herbs, and supplements you take in addition to that. If you let other people know about your medical profile, it will make it easier for you to avoid potentially embarrassing situations.

Nitrates

Cialis is not something you should use if you are already using a prescription medication that is classified as a nitrate. When Cialis is used in conjunction with nitrates, the user runs the risk of having a potentially life-threatening decrease in blood pressure. Some examples of nitrates include the following:

- Nitroglycerin.
- Isosorbide mononitrate (Monoket).

- Isosorbide dinitrate (Isordil).

It is possible that your doctor will opt to give you a nitrate if it has been at least 48 hours since you took the previous dose of Cialis. In the event that you are having pain in your chest and your life is in jeopardy, this might be one of the scenarios that play out. After the nitrate has been given to you, your doctor will most likely keep a tight watch on you in order to monitor your blood pressure and make sure it does not drop to an unsafely low level.

Alpha-blockers

Cialis, along with other medications belonging to the family of pharmaceuticals known as alpha-blockers, has the ability to bring the patient's blood pressure down. Because of this, taking these two medications at the same time may result in an even more significant drop in blood pressure. If you have a disease known as benign prostatic hyperplasia (BPH) and are also on a medicine known as an alpha-blocker, Cialis is not something that you should take. In addition, if you are taking an alpha-blocker and suffer from erectile dysfunction (ED), your doctor would most likely limit the quantity of Cialis you take. This is because the two conditions interact negatively with each other. The following are some examples of drugs that are considered alpha-blockers:

- Tamsulosin (Flomax).
- Alfuzosin (Uroxatral).
- Doxazosin (Cardura).

Before starting therapy with Cialis, it is important that you discuss all of the medications, including alpha-blockers that you are already taking with your primary care physician. If you have any concerns or questions regarding probable harmful effects caused by drug interactions, you should discuss them with either your primary care physician or a pharmacist.

Medications those can bring the patient's blood pressure down.

There is a possibility that taking Cialis will result in a drop in your blood pressure. If you are currently taking other drugs prescribed to decrease your blood pressure, using Cialis on top of those other medications may cause your blood pressure to drop even more than it has already been lowered by the other medications. Metoprolol (Toprol XL, Lopressor), amlodipine (Norvasc), and enalapril are only few of the medications in use for the treatment of significant arterial pressure. Other medications like these may also be utilized (Vasotec).

Before starting treatment with Cialis, it is important that you let your healthcare practitioner know if you are currently taking any drugs for blood pressure. They could begin you on a lower dose of Cialis or increase the number of times you are monitored. Both of these options are available.

Medications to treat heartburn

If you are taking Cialis and treating heartburn with antacids, you should be aware that this might cause the body to absorb less of the Cialis. This is extremely significant if you are taking both medications. It is likely that you may not get the full dose of Cialis because of this, and consequently, the medicine may not be as effective in treating your erectile dysfunction (ED) or the symptoms of benign prostatic hyperplasia (BPH). Examples of antacids include:

- Calcium carbonate (Tums).
- Aluminum hydroxide/magnesium hydroxide (Mylanta).

Before commencing therapy with Cialis, inform your doctor if you are currently using any antacids. If your condition requires you to take prescription medications, you and your physician should have a conversation about how far apart the doses of each medication should be taken from one another.

CYP3A4 enzyme inhibitor

Within your body is an enzyme known as CYP3A4, which is found in your liver. An enzyme is a kind of protein that acts as a catalyst for chemical processes that take place within the body. Certain medications have the capacity to block the activity of this enzyme, which means that they may interrupt its normal function. This might put your health in peril and increase the possibility that Cialis will cause you to encounter side effects that you do not desire. The following is a list of some drugs that are examples of those that may inhibit CYP3A4 from completing its job:

- Ketoconazole.
- Itraconazole (Sporanox) (Sporanox).
- Erythromycin (Ery-Tab) (Ery-Tab).
- Ritonavir (Norvir).

Before starting therapy with Cialis, it is essential to have a conversation with your primary care physician about any other drugs that you are already taking. They will be able to determine whether or not the drugs in issue are CYP3A4 inhibitors, as well as whether or not Cialis may be impacted by using them.

Inducers of CYP3A4 activity

Cialis is broken down in the liver by an enzyme known as CYP3A4, which is responsible for this process. It is possible for some drugs to stimulate (increase the activity of) the enzyme CYP3A4, causing it to operate at a rate that is either higher than normal or much quicker than usual. This suggests that the medication Cialis may not have the intended impact on you since your body may be breaking it down faster than it should be. The following pharmaceuticals are some examples of those that are known to induce CYP3A4:

- Rifampin.
- Carbamazepine.
- Phenytoin.
- Phenobarbital.

They will be able to determine whether or not the drugs in issue are CYP3A4 inducers and whether or not Cialis might possibly be impacted by them. It is conceivable that your doctor may propose switching to a different medication in order to treat either your erectile dysfunction (ED) or the symptoms of your BPH. Alternatively, he may treat both conditions at the same time.

Agents that stimulate the action of guanylate cyclase

Patients who are also taking a drug that is classified as a guanylate cyclase stimulator should not use Cialis, since doing so might increase the risk of serious side effects. It is common practice to provide medication of this kind to patients who have been diagnosed with pulmonary hypertension in order to treat their condition (a type of high blood pressure in your lungs). It is conceivable that if you use Cialis together with a guanylate cyclase stimulator, your blood pressure will drop to a dangerous level. This may happen if your blood pressure values drop too low.

The condition known as pulmonary arterial hypertension can occur in the arteries of the lungs themselves (pulmonary hypertension), or it can occur in the lungs themselves as a result of a blood clot in the lungs. This medicine may be used to treat pulmonary hypertension (PH), which is also known as PAH.

Before commencing therapy with Cialis, it is most important to have a talk with your doctor about any other medications for the treatment of pulmonary hypertension that you are already taking. If you are currently using riociguat, your doctor will probably recommend that you switch to a different medication to treat either your erectile dysfunction (ED) symptoms or your BPH symptoms, or both, depending on which condition you are trying to treat.

Alcohol

Both Cialis and alcohol have the ability to bring one's blood pressure down to a lower level. Since this is the case, if you drink alcohol while taking this medication, it is highly recommended that you cut down on the quantity of alcohol that you consume. It is conceivable that this will assist in preventing your blood pressure from dropping to levels that might be considered dangerously low.

Grapefruit

While you are under the influence of Cialis, it is highly advised that you avoid consuming grapefruit in any form, including eating grapefruit and drinking grapefruit juice. Within your body is an enzyme known as CYP3A4, which is found in your liver. The enzyme is impeded from doing its activity when grapefruit is present. This might potentially endanger your health and increase the risk that Cialis will cause you to encounter unwelcome side effects.

Chapter 4: Mechanism of Action

How does Cialis Work?

The relaxation of smooth muscle may be the most typical therapeutic effect that tadalafil, which is a selective phosphodiesterase-5 (PDE5) inhibitor, may have. Tadalafil is given to people who suffer from pulmonary arterial hypertension in addition to erectile dysfunction so that they might improve their sexual performance. Erectile dysfunction, more often referred to as ED, may be caused by a wide range of factors, some of which are psychogenic, some are neurogenic, some are vasculogenic, some are iatrogenic, and others are endocrine in origin. A malfunction in the relaxation of the penile smooth muscle may be generated when these elements are present by either a disruption in the neural signaling or a direct influence on the smooth muscle cells of the penile sphincter. Neurons that are neither adrenergic nor possess cholinergic receptors will open their gates and release some nitric oxide when the body is in a state of sexual desire. The enzyme known as guanylate cyclase is able to transform guanosine triphosphate into cyclic guanosine monophosphate, and it becomes more active when nitric oxide is present. This is because nitric oxide stimulates the enzyme (cGMP). In a signaling cascade, it is cGMP that is ultimately responsible for the activation of the cGMP-dependent kinase (PKG). This, in turn, leads to the activation of K+ channels, which, in turn, leads to the inhibition of Ca2+ channels, which, in turn, leads to the inhibition of platelet activation, which, in turn, leads to the inhibition of smooth muscle cell growth, which simultaneously triggers death. The chain of events continues until death is triggered. PDE5 is the enzyme that is responsible for modulating the consequences of this signal cascade in a negative manner. The enzyme known as PDE5 is the one that is responsible for the conversion of cGMP into GMP. It does this by severing the phosphodiester link that is accountable for keeping it jointly. Inhibiting PDE5 is how Tadalafil achieves its therapeutic effect, which ultimately results in an increase in signaling all the way down the PKG cascade. A reduction in the quantity of calcium ions enters the smooth muscle cells whenever there is an increase in sexual desire. Because of this relaxation of the smooth muscle, blood is able to fill the corpus cavernosum, which ultimately leads to an erection.

A rise in blood pressure in the pulmonary arteries is one of the defining characteristics of pulmonary arterial hypertension (PAH), which is also known by its acronym. This rise in blood pressure in the pulmonary arteries may be traced back to a variety of distinct mechanisms, all of which begin from endothelial dysfunction. As a result, the source of this elevation in blood pressure in the pulmonary arteries can be determined. Vasodilatory signaling may be hampered when NO and prostacyclin synthesis is reduced, but vasoconstrictive signaling may be enhanced when endothelin-1 and thromboxane production are increased. This factor causes an increase in blood pressure, which in turn leads to a decrease in the capacity for gas exchange, as well as an increase in the afterload that is imposed on the right ventricle of the heart. This not only causes symptoms such as shortness of breath, fatigue, and lightheadedness, but it also leads to failure of the right side of the heart. The therapeutic impact of tadalafil in PAH is achieved in the same way as it is in the treatment of erectile dysfunction; specifically, it does this by increasing NO-cGMP signaling, which in turn causes relaxation of smooth muscle. This is the same process that is at play when a man has trouble maintaining an erection.

To elaborate, tadalafil is one of the treatment choices that may be taken into consideration for BPH. Urinary dysfunction is an indication that benign prostatic hyperplasia is present. Medication is one option for the treatment of urinary dysfunction (BPH). Because of the enlarged prostate, urine is impossible to pass through the urethra in a natural and unobstructed manner. Because of this, even after the bladder has been partially emptied, it will continue to hold a greater amount of pee than normal. It does not seem that tadalafil causes a relaxation of the smooth muscle in the prostate, which would be the mechanism via which it would exercise its curative benefits on the disease. It is possible that it achieves its effect by combining a number of different mechanisms, such as an improvement in oxygenation and a reduction in inflammation, both of which lead to a reduction in tissue remodeling, as well as a suppression of cell proliferation achieved via the cGMP cascade. It is also feasible that it achieves its effect through a conjunction of these mechanisms. It is also conceivable that it accomplishes its action simply via the cGMP cascade, which is an alternative explanation.

Since PDE6 is located in the eye and is necessary for color vision, the lower affinity that other PDE5 inhibitors have for PDE6 may explain why there is a lower frequency of visual adverse effects.

Duration

The findings of certain studies indicate that the medicine could start to have an impact on the body as soon as a half an hour has elapsed after the prescribed dose has been administered to the body. However, the length of time it takes before you start to feel the effects of the therapy may range anywhere from three to six hours depending on the individual who is taking the drug. After the initial dose of Cialis is taken, the drug does not begin to exert its full effect for around two hours. This is the amount of time that must pass before you will be able to get the maximum concentration of the drug that is potentially possible in your body. At this stage, the medication should have reached its maximum effectiveness, making it possible for it to effectively cure your erectile dysfunction (ED), the symptoms of BPH, or both illnesses.

Pharmacodynamics

The therapeutic impact that tadalafil has on erectile dysfunction is achieved by improving the smooth muscle relaxation in the penis that is dependent on sexual stimulation. The corpus cavernosum is able to get filled with blood as a consequence of this, which finally results in an erection. PAH is distinguished by the relaxation of smooth muscles within the pulmonary vasculature, which results in the development of vasodilation. In turn, this vasodilation lowers the blood pressure inside the pulmonary arteries, which is a beneficial effect. Tadalafil may limit the proliferation of smooth muscle cells in patients who have benign prostatic hyperplasia (BPH). This may result in a smaller prostate and relief from the structural obstruction that is the underlying cause of urinary symptoms associated with BPH. Tadalafil may also lead to a reduction in the risk of adverse events. It is possible that the reduced occurrence of ocular adverse effects is because tadalafil has a weaker affinity for PDE6 in contrast to other PDE5 inhibitors. Only additional researches may demonstrate it.

Pharmacokinetics

After a single dose of Cialis, the peak concentration (Cmax) might occur anywhere from 30 minutes to 6 hours after taking the medication. After an injection, the maximum concentration of the drug, or Cmax, is typically attained two hours later. After five days of taking the once-daily dosage, a stable state is achieved and may be kept up.

A volume of distribution of around 63 liters may be expected with Cialis. It is estimated that bound proteins account for around 94% of its total mass.

Following this step, methylation and glucuronidation take place, which ultimately leads to the production of methylcatechol glucuronide, which is a metabolized product.

Following this, Cialis is expelled from the body, with 61% of it being discovered in the feces and 36% of it being discovered in the urine.

Half-life: Cialis has an extended half-life of approximately 17.5 hours, significantly longer than other PDE5 inhibitors, making it effective for up to 36 hours after administration. This property earned Cialis the nickname "the weekend pill".

Chapter 5: Dosage and Side Effects

The Right Dosage and Timing is Fundamental

Your doctor will tailor the dosage of Cialis that he or she prescribes for you to take depending on a wide variety of factors. The following are some of them:

- Your age.
- Any other medical situation you may have.
- The type and seriousness of the problem you are using Cialis to treat.
- How often you take Cialis, and how much you take each time you take it are all important factors to consider.

The majority of the time, your medical professional will start the therapy with a very low dosage. After then, they will continue to make changes to it over the course of time in order to arrive at a total that is suitable for you. In the end, your doctor will prescribe the minimum effective dosage of the medication that will still have the desired effect.

Your physician may advise you to begin therapy with Cialis at a low dose if you have a medical condition that affects particular organs in your body, such as kidney or liver problems. This is done to make certain that the medication will not have a negative interaction with any of the other conditions that you suffer from. The information that is presented in the following sections offers a description of dosages that are often used or proposed. However, be sure to take the dosage that your doctor or other medical practitioner has recommended for you to take. Your doctor will determine the appropriate dosage for you depending on your specific needs by looking at a number of factors.

Dosage for Erectile Dysfunction

If your physician has recommended that you only use Cialis when absolutely essential to treat ED, the standard dosage is 10 milligrams, which should be taken 30 minutes before participating in sexual activity. It may be necessary to reduce the dose of the medication to 5 mg if it has an excessively noticeable impact. After this, the dose will be 10 mg, which is 10 mg more than its prior amount. In the event that your physician thinks that the 10-mg dose of Cialis is not generating the expected effects, the quantity may be raised to 20 mg.

At the very most, you should only take Cialis once every twenty-four hours. In clinical testing, a single dose of Cialis was proven to be helpful in treating symptoms of erectile dysfunction (ED) for a period of up to 36 hours. If you are just taking the prescribed medication when you really need it, then you probably do not need to take it on a daily basis. It is of the highest essential that you take exactly the amount of Cialis that has been recommended by the medical practitioner who is treating you. If you believe that you need a higher amount of the drug than what you are now taking, you should talk to your healthcare provider before increasing your dosage on your own.

Taking Cialis once a day

In addition, Cialis may be used once daily as a treatment for erectile dysfunction (ED). In this particular scenario, the typical beginning dosage is 2.5 mg taken once a day. If your doctor determines that the present quantity of medication you are taking for the treatment of your erectile dysfunction is not successful enough, he or she may choose to increase your daily dosage to 5 mg (ED). In addition, if your doctor recommends that you use Cialis daily, you should be sure to take the medicine at around the same time each day. This represents a guarantee that the drug has the required effect. It is not necessary for you to take Cialis before participating in sexual activity, provided that your doctor has not ordered you to use the medicine on an as-needed basis. This is the situation where you may not require taking the medication.

It is very critical that you just take the proper dose of Cialis as recommended by your physician. This is the sole manner to ascertain that you get the desired results from this medication. If you believe that you need a higher amount of the drug than what you are now taking, you should talk to your healthcare provider before increasing your dosage on your own.

Higher Dosages of Cialis

It is unknown what harmful effects may be associated with taking such a large dosage since there have been no studies done on doses that are greater than 20 milligrams per day.

For instance, if you take your "as required" dosage of 20 milligrams twice a day, you would end up taking in a total of 40 milligrams of the medicine over the course of a day. This number is significantly more than what is considered to be safe, and it has the potential to induce a range of highly dangerous adverse effects, including a drop in blood pressure, which is only one of the many possible side effects.

Main Side Effects

The potential adverse effects of Cialis might vary from being completely safe to being quite dangerous. The following list provides specific examples of some of the most typical unfavorable effects that some users of Cialis have reported while using the medication. It is possible that the topic listed will not cover every possible adverse response that might take place. Have a conversation about the possible adverse effects that taking Cialis might have on your body with your primary care physician, your pharmacist, or both. They will be able to provide you guidance on how to manage any unpleasant side effect that may arise as a result of taking the medication. Users of Cialis may encounter any or all of the following mild side effects:

- Aches and pains in the head, stomach, and back.
- Flushing of the face, pain in the muscles and a congested nose (warmth and redness in your skin).
- Either your arms or your legs are giving you trouble.

There is a possibility that the bulk of these unintended effects may go away in a couple of days or weeks at the very most. You should talk to either your doctor or your pharmacist if the symptoms continue or become worse or if they do not go away altogether. Although Cialis has been known to have severe side effects on occasion, this is not an everyday occurrence. In the event that you are suffering significant unfavorable consequences, you need to get in touch with your doctor as soon as you can. If you think that your symptoms are extremely critical or if you feel you may be suffering a medical emergency, you should contact 911 as soon as possible. The following is a list of instances of major side effects, as well as the symptoms that they cause:

- Hearing impairments caused by this condition.
- Discrepancies in hearing ability.
- A difficulty in hearing.
- You are experiencing dizziness and sounds coming from your ears.

While taking this drug, you may be concerned about the likelihood of experiencing a number of undesirable side effects. The following are some suggestions on the potential adverse effects of using this medicine.

Reactions brought on by allergic reactions

It is possible for some people to have a negative reaction after taking Cialis, just as it is the case with most drugs. Some of the people who took part in the clinical trials of Cialis reported having allergic reactions, although the specific number of people who did so was not made public. Among the allergic reactions there was a severe rash, as well as conditions that damage the skin, such Stevens-Johnson syndrome. The following is a list of symptoms that may accompany an allergic response that is considered to be mild:

- Skin rash
- Itching
- Flushing of the skin

It is quite unlikely for someone to have a more severe allergic reaction, but it is not impossible. The following is a list of symptoms that may be observed in conjunction with a severe allergic reaction:

- A swelling that develops under the surface of your skin and most often appears in your eyelids, lips, hands, or feet.
- The tongue, mouth, or throat may swell, and breathing may become difficult.
- Further symptoms include these.

In the event that you get a severe allergic reaction after using Cialis, you need to get in touch with your doctor as quickly as you can. If your symptoms seem to be life threatening or if you feel you may be suffering a medical emergency, you should contact your doctor as soon as possible.

Headache

Cialis is known to have many possible negative side effects, and headaches are one of those impacts. During clinical testing, anyone of the following might take place, depending on the illness or condition being evaluated and treated:

- Those who took Cialis reported having headaches at a rate ranging from 3% to 15% of all users.
- Those who were given a placebo reported experiencing headaches at a rate ranging from 2.3 percent to 5 percent.
- If you find that taking Cialis is giving you headaches that are very bothersome, you should analyze the topic with your doctor. They may be able to provide some recommendations that will make the pain produced by this side effect more bearable.

Alterations to one's blood pressure

Taking Cialis may cause your blood pressure to fluctuate, which is a potential adverse effect. While using this medicine, most people evidence low blood pressure. However, elevated blood pressure is a possibility as well.

A lowering in the blood pressure.

In clinical studies, participants' blood pressure was measured before and after they took 20 milligrams of Cialis or a placebo. When compared to the placebo group, those who took Cialis saw a reduction in their blood pressure that was an average of 1.6/0.8 mm Hg greater. If you use Cialis in conjunction with other drugs that have the ability to bring down your blood pressure, the likelihood of your blood pressure going down will increase. If you evidence a low blood pressure, including the following:

- Dizziness
- Eyesight that is hazy
- Fainting

Inform your healthcare provider right away when experiencing any of these side effects while taking Cialis. They will assist in determining which the cause of the low blood pressure is and find the most suitable therapy for it.

Elevated levels of blood pressure.

There is a possibility, although a small one, that Cialis may raise your blood pressure. People who used Cialis once daily for erectile dysfunction were the only ones who reported experiencing this particular adverse effect. Depending on the ailment that was being treated, during this experiment:

- One percent to three percent of those who took the drug had elevated blood pressure as a side effect.
- No one who took a sugar pill had elevated blood pressure after taking the placebo.

You should see your physician as soon as possible if you have any symptoms of high blood pressure, including chest discomfort or headaches. They will assist in determining what the cause of the rise in blood pressure is and find the most suitable therapy for it.

Back pain

Cialis is known to cause a frequent adverse effect known as back discomfort. In clinical studies, patients with back pain reported the following conditions, depending on the illness being treated:

- 2% to 6% of patients who used Cialis reported adverse events.

- 1% to 3% of those who were given a placebo reported adverse events.

Back discomfort is a common side effect of Cialis, and it often begins between 12 and 24 hours after taking the medication. After taking your dosage for back pain, you should get relief within two days, on average.

Talk to your healthcare provider if the back discomfort you experience while taking Cialis is troublesome or if it does not go away as prescribed. They are surely able to give you any indication for alleviating the discomfort caused by this side effect. Your doctor may do further diagnostic tests, in order to be able to ascertain the origin of your discomfort.

Heartburn

Cialis is known to cause a frequent adverse effect known as heartburn. In clinical studies, heartburn occurred in a variety of patients based on the ailment being treated, including but not limited to the following:

- Cialis users made about 1% to 10% of the total population.
- 0.2% to 2% of those who received a placebo reported feeling any different.

Discuss with your physician if you get heartburn during the therapy with Cialis that is severe or causes you discomfort. They will surely recommend other treatments for this unwanted side effect.

Prolonged erection

While using Cialis, it is possible to have a sustained erection that lasts longer than four hours. In the clinical testing, it has not been possible to record how many of the people engaged had a sustained erection. This adverse consequence may result in priapism, which means a painful erection that lasts longer than four hours. Because it has the potential to inflict irreversible damage to the penis, such as the inability to have erections at all, it is classified as an emergency. Immediately see a medical professional or go to the emergency room if you take Cialis and, consequently, your erection lasts for more than four hours. It is necessary to start the treatment at the earliest possible for the extended erection so that there is no permanent harm caused by it.

Loss of ability to see

Cialis has a very low risk of causing vision loss in either one eye or both eyes; however, this risk is very low. In the clinical testing, it has not been possible to record how many people had a loss of eyesight. In addition, it is unknown if the usage of Cialis was the cause of the loss of eyesight or whether other variables had a role. If you have any changes in your eyesight while using Cialis, such as reduced vision or loss of vision, you should contact your doctor as soon as possible. They will assist in determining what is causing the change in eyesight as well as the most effective treatment option for it.

Chapter 6: Frequently Asked Questions

1. Does Cialis really work?

In fact, the Cialis brand has been granted the green light for sale by the Food and Drug Administration (FDA). In order for the FDA to give its blessing to a pharmaceutical product, the drug in issue must first be tested to see whether it is both safe and effective. Cialis has been demonstrated to be both reliable and efficacious in clinical tests for the treatment of both ED and BPH. ED refers to erectile dysfunction, while BPH refers to benign prostatic hyperplasia.

2. Is there a difference between Cialis and Viagra?

The biggest difference between Viagra and Cialis is how long the effects of each prescription continue to work inside of a person's body after they have been taken. Users of Viagra have plenty of time to engage in sexual activity several times if they so want since the effects of the medication may last anywhere from four to six hours. One pill of Cialis, on the other hand, has the potential to help you get and keep an erection for as long as 36 hours after you take it.

3. What is the most appropriate way to take Cialis?

If you are only going to use Cialis when you really need it, wait at least a half an hour after taking it before indulging in sexual activity. If your physician has suggested that you take Cialis regularly, it is imperative that you maintain the correct time of intake every day. Because of this, the quantity of Cialis that is present in your body will remain stable.

4. Which is better between Cialis, Viagra and Levitra for longer performance?

Cialis has an advantage over Viagra and Levitra owing to the fact that its effects may be felt for a much longer amount of time, up to 36 hours, whilst the effects of Viagra and Levitra only last for 4-5 hours at a time.

5. Can I take Cialis and Viagra together?

The usage of Cialis and Viagra at the same time is not something that is encouraged. Combining them not only will not relieve the symptoms of erectile dysfunction (ED), but it will also put the user's health in jeopardy. Ask your doctor about any problem you might face about the causes of your ED. In some cases, the most effective strategy to aid in the treatment of ED symptoms is to combine the use of medication with changes in one's way of life. This is one of the most successful ways.

6. Do you require a prescription to take Cialis?

It is not possible to purchase Cialis or any other medication for erectile dysfunction over the counter. On the other hand, if you have erectile dysfunction, getting a prescription for Cialis, Viagra, or any of the other ED medicines is a process that may be completed in a manner that is considered very simple.

7. Does Cialis affect sperm quality

Tadalafil improves the quality of the seminal fluid as well as the sperm cells. Specifically, it raises the volume of the seminal fluid, the percentage of nemasperms, and the motility of the sperm.

8. How long does Cialis take to be effective?

It might take anywhere from thirty to sixty minutes for the anti-impotence medication tadalafil to start functioning successfully against erectile dysfunction. This time limit is not absolute. You only need to take it once per day, and you should do it at least half an hour before you plan to engage in any kind of sexual activity.

9. Can women take Cialis?

Cialis has not been approved for use in the treatment of sexual dysfunction in females, and there has not been nearly enough research done to determine whether the medication is both effective and safe for people who have reproductive organs that are female.

10. Does Cialis lower the blood pressure?

There is a possibility that Cialis will induce a very little reduction in blood pressure. The vast majority of men will not have any problems because of this, but the effect that Cialis has on blood pressure may be exaggerated if it is used in combination with another prescription that includes nitrates. This is something that most men will not have to worry about. Nitrates are one of the treatments that patients who suffer from angina are often advised to undergo by their attending physicians.

Conclusion

Cialis (tadalafil) has emerged as a cornerstone treatment for erectile dysfunction (ED), benign prostatic hyperplasia (BPH), and pulmonary arterial hypertension (PAH), revolutionizing how these conditions are managed. Its unique pharmacological properties, particularly its extended half-life and targeted inhibition of phosphodiesterase type 5 (PDE5), have provided patients with greater flexibility, efficacy, and convenience. Unlike earlier treatments for ED, Cialis offers a longer duration of action—up to 36 hours—allowing for increased spontaneity in sexual activity and reducing the anxiety associated with timed dosing. Its proven efficacy in treating BPH and PAH further underscores the drug's versatility and the importance of PDE5 inhibition in vascular health beyond sexual function.

Throughout this book, we have explored not only the mechanism by which Cialis operates but also its pharmacokinetics, therapeutic uses, and the critical safety considerations that ensure its effective use. As with any medication, understanding the potential side effects, drug interactions, and contraindications is crucial for healthcare providers and patients alike. The ability of Cialis to enhance quality of life while maintaining a favorable safety profile has made it one of the most trusted therapies for conditions involving vascular smooth muscle dysfunction.

Cialis represents more than just a treatment for ED; it highlights the power of advancements in pharmacology to address a range of health issues, expanding therapeutic options for patients worldwide. Moving forward, the success of tadalafil opens the door for continued research and innovation in vascular-related therapies, offering hope for future advancements that may improve patient outcomes even further.

In conclusion, Cialis stands as a testament to modern medicine's ability to not only treat conditions like erectile dysfunction but to profoundly impact overall well-being, providing a new level of confidence, intimacy, and vitality for those who use it.

Printed by
Youcanprint

www.ingramcontent.com/pod-product-compliance
Lightning Source LLC
LaVergne TN
LVHW022016270125
802331LV00007B/306